Penmanship and Fine Lettering
A Designer's Resource

D1616280

Preface

Let Penmanship, that lovely art,
To please the eye, instruct the heart,
Attention claim from every youth,
Attach'd to virtue and to truth.
                              -Ezra Eastman, 1821

This volume is a reprint of two books: *Real Pen Work*, published in 1881 by Knowles & Maxim of Pittsfield, Massachusetts; and *Atkinson Sign Painting: A Complete Manual*, published in 1915 by Frederick J. Drake & Company of Chicago. Both books have been edited, with extraneous plates removed. Some pages showing alphabets and rough sketches for signs have been deleted from the Atkinson book due to space limitations.

Copyright © 1997 by John Mendenhall
laszlo.libart.calpoly.edu

All rights reserved. This book may not be reproduced, stored in a retrieval system, or transmitted in any form or by any means without prior permission of the publisher.

ISBN: 0-88108-202-3
LCCN: 97-073401

Printed in the United States of America

Published by:
Art Direction Book Company, Incorporated
456 Glenbrook Road
Glenbrook, Connecticut 06906

The art of penmanship was popularized throughout the 19th century in America and was considered so important for American youth to learn that it was taught in all public and business schools. The art of elegant handwriting was practiced by a wide variety of "writing masters" who were also influential in their teachings. John Jenkins, Henry Dean, William Milns, Jacob Perkins, James Carver, and Benjamin Rand were just a few of many penmen who lived and taught in the Boston and Philadelphia areas in the mid–1800s.

From 1810 it became increasingly important that all businessmen be proficient in the craft of fine handwriting. Business correspondence, check writing, and invoices all utilized ably written scripts that were often embellished with flourishes and other fancy touches. Flourishing was considered an integral part of elegant penmanship, and was created by moving the hand and pen at a constant speed, swinging "bold and free" circular rhythms.

Mastery of an elegant hand was synonymous with taste and refinement in American society. An intelligent citizen was expected to go through the rigorous lessons required for perfection of the art. One famous penman was Benjamin Franklin Foster, an accountant and teacher of writing at the Albany Female Academy in New York in the 1830s. He developed the Carstairian system of writing, which was reviewed in the *American Annals of Education*:

"The fundamental principle of this system is to transfer to writing the free movement of design. For this purpose, the pupil is first taught to form letters simply by the movement of *the arm*, without any sustaining point; and to secure this, the fingers are tied, so as to be incapable of motion, and the arm is not allowed to touch the table. As soon as the perfect command of the arm is acquired in this manner, the learner is allowed to rest the part near the elbow on the table, and taught to use the fore arm. His fingers are then untied, and he is allowed to avail himself of their movements in rendering his letters more accurate or delicate in their forms."

Real Pen Work was published as a self-help book for those who wished to learn penmanship on their own. Besides giving instructions on sitting and holding the pen, it offered the reader plates that could be copied via the transfer process. Using this method the student could make their own carbon paper for tracing designs.

By the end of the 19th century the formalities of individual penmanship had spread to the graphic arts, where publicity designers and sign painters incorporated many of its principles in creating such things as show cards, letterheads, and advertisements. The popularity of Art Nouveau, with its elegant floral line work, was also a major influence on these craftsmen at this time.

One of the most highly respected handletterers of the era was Frank A. Atkinson, a sign painter and show card artist of incredible skill. His studio was located in Chicago, a city that saw rapid industrialization at the turn of the century. Sign painters such as Atkinson were in high demand, as businesses of all types required attractive signs that would appeal to the crowds passing by on the streets.

In 1915 he prepared a book on the subject, *Atkinson Sign Painting: A Complete Manual*, that showcased numerous examples of work done by himself and his contemporaries. The text of the book gave detailed instructions on preparing artwork for signs, brush lettering, gilding, and mixing paints. For those who are interested, it can be accessed at: laszlo.libart.calpoly.edu/atkinson.

Both books give insight into the vanishing art of handlettering. In this age of digital type and e–mail, this reprint will hopefully be an inspiring resource for those who wish to explore a "new" approach in their own professional work.

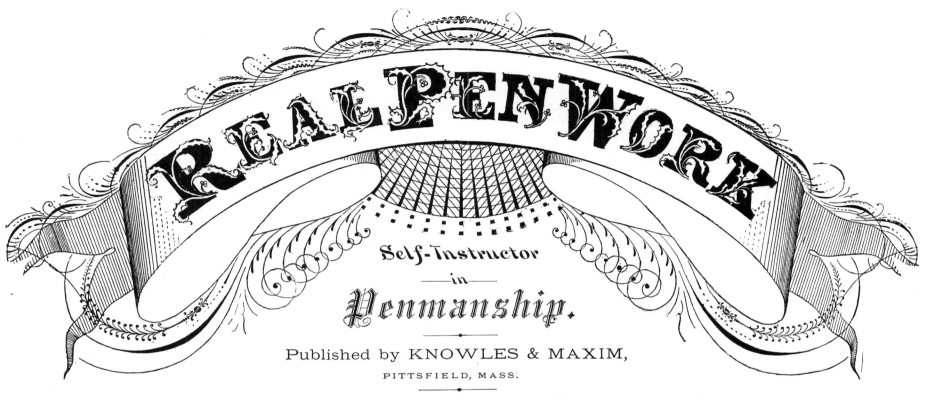

REAL PEN WORK

Self-Instructor

in

Penmanship.

Published by KNOWLES & MAXIM,

PITTSFIELD, MASS.

PRICE, ONE DOLLAR PER COPY.

GREATEST MEANS EVER KNOWN FOR LEARNING TO WRITE AN ELEGANT HAND.

NOTHING LIKE IT EVER PUBLISHED BEFORE.

SOMETHING ENTIRELY NEW.   SOMETHING THAT EVERYBODY WANTS.   SOMETHING THAT HAS THE MOST ENTHRALLING INTEREST FOR ALL.

The Real Pen-Work Self-Instructor in Penmanship

Contains more Copies, more Ornamental Work, and more and better Instructions, for learning the Whole Art of Penmanship without a teacher, than any other work ever published in the World. Everything is explained in such a plain and simple way, that any one, no matter how difficult writing may naturally be to him, can learn to write a beautiful hand in an incredibly short time.

NO OTHER PUBLISHERS IN THE WORLD ARE GIVING THE PEOPLE AS MUCH FOR THE MONEY.   NOTHING LIKE IT EVER KNOWN BEFORE.

The Largest and most elegantly Illustrated Work on the subject of Penmanship ever published in the World. Expert Penmen and Men of Learning everywhere, all admit that the Real Pen-Work Self-Instructor is the greatest means ever known for learning to write an elegant hand.

Copyrighted 1881, by KNOWLES & MAXIM, Publishers, Pittsfield, Mass.

INTRODUCTION

TO THE

Real Pen-Work Self-Instructor in Penmanship,

PUBLISHED BY

KNOWLES & MAXIM,

PITTSFIELD, MASS.

PRICE, ONE DOLLAR PER COPY.

GREATEST MEANS EVER KNOWN FOR LEARNING TO WRITE AN ELEGANT HAND.

THIS BOOK,

THE REAL PEN-WORK SELF-INSTRUCTOR IN PENMANSHIP,

is by far the largest and most elegantly illustrated work on the subject of Penmanship ever published. Full of the most beautiful writing, pen-drawing and flourishing that could be produced by the combined efforts of the very best Penmen and Pen Artists in the world.

THE BEST OF ALL

that was ever thought of by all the very best Writers and Penmen who ever lived, to make it easy to learn to write, to learn all the different and *most beautiful* styles of elegant Writing and Ornamental Penmanship, is contained in the Real Pen-Work Self-Instructor. It is full of the prettiest things ever done with a pen. Full of perfect real Written Copies. And it contains full and complete instructions for learning the whole art of penmanship without a teacher.

IT TEACHES AND SHOWS YOU

just how to go to work to learn to write nicely, and just how to make everything that can be thought or conceived of that is beautiful or desirable to do

with a pen. Everything is made so plain and simple and easy, that no one can fail to understand it all, and no one can fail to learn to write an elegant hand from the Self-Instructor, in a very short time, if he will only try. Nothing has been neglected. Everything is explained in such a plain and simple way, that no one can fail to understand it all. As strange as it may seem, any one, young or old, even the dullest scholar, if he will try, can learn from the Self-Instructor to write an elegant hand in only a few weeks.

HOW WE CAME TO PUBLISH THE

REAL PEN-WORK SELF-INSTRUCTOR IN PENMANSHIP.

Some three years since our attention was called to a new and ingenious process called Photo-Electrographing, by which process all kinds of writing and pen-work can be reproduced on paper, so perfect and exact, that the reproduction or Photo-Electrograph cannot be told from the original writing, even by the person who wrote it. We thoroughly tested the process by having some of our own writing reproduced, and when the originals, along with several of the Photo-Electro-

graphs, were afterwards shown us, we failed to select the originals, or the ones we had done with a pen, from the others.

We fully realized, from the first, the great value of this discovery. We saw at once, that by reproducing real pen-work by this process, we could publish a Self-Instructor in Penmanship, and give such an immense amount and variety of elegant writing, pen-lettering, flourishing, scrolling and drawing, at so small a cost, that the work would take the people by surprise everywhere, and sell to nearly every family in the civilized world. Therefore we determined, at once, to take advantage of the Photo-Electrographing process, and publish a work, which should be in every particular a Real Pen-Work Self-Instructor in Penmanship.

We immediately went to work in earnest, preparing for the publication of the Real Pen-Work Self-Instructor in Penmanship.

Of course, the most important thing to be done was to obtain the Pen-Work. We resolved to employ the very best penmen and pen artists in the world to set all the copies and do all the writing and drawing for the work. In order to get the very best writing done, and the very best specimens of plain and ornamental penmanship, we consulted, either by letter or in person, nearly all the best penman and pen artists in the world. Regardless of cost we purchased of each of them the finest and best designs of both plain and ornamental penmanship, writing and drawing that they were able to execute.

Many of the designs cost a very large sum, but they were purchased, as we determined to have nothing but the best.

After nearly eleven months of constant labor and research, we succeeded in securing a collection of fine writing, pen-lettering, flourishing, scrolling and drawing, the beauty and variety of which is beyond all power to describe.

This entire collection, with the addition of several designs of our own execution, has been inserted in the Real Pen-Work Self-Instructor, by the Photo-Electrographing process.

These Photo-Electrographs are so perfect in every case that they cannot possibly be told from the original pen and ink work.

As soon as we had obtained all the pen-work that we desired, we employed three of the most eminent educational men in America, to assist us in preparing the work for publication. And finally, about one year ago, we completed and published the Real Pen-Work-Self Instructor in Penmanship. And to-day, this immense work stands alone, as much ahead of any other work ever published on penmanship as Webster's Unabridged Dictionary is ahead of the definitions in a child's second reader.

THE SUCCESS OF THE WORK IS WONDERFUL.

We have spared no time, no labor, no expense, to make the Self-Instructor just what it is, just what the people want, and the result is nothing short of

WONDERFUL SUCCESS.

We realized from the first the great value of the work to the people. We expected immense success. We predicted a sale of twenty thousand copies the first year. But when we state that, instead of twenty thousand, the sale has reached the enormous number of over one hundred thousand copies the first year, you can get some idea of the unbounded satisfaction that the Self-Instructor must be giving.

We are proud of the work and its success. We have a right to be, for never before was there anything ever known to sell like the Real Pen-Work Self-Instructor, in the history of the whole great publishing business.

The great secret of how we can afford to give so much for the money, as we have already explained, is the Photo-Electrographing process.

But even with the immense advantage of using this valuable process, we never could sell the Self-Instructor for so low a price as we do, except from the fact that we are selling such immense numbers.

One hundred thousand copies have been sold by our agents during the last year, and we have every reason to believe that during the next year, we shall not sell less than a million copies.

These are enormous sales, unparalleled in the history of the publishing business. And yet it is not surprising. Everybody has a great desire to learn to write an elegant hand.

There has always been an immense demand for a perfect Self-Instructor in Penmanship. And since the publication of the Real Pen-Work Self-Instructor, which makes it so easy to learn to write an elegant hand in so short a time, no one hesitates, all are ready to buy as soon as they see or hear of the work.

LOOK THE SELF-INSTRUCTOR THROUGH

And you will see a greater variety, and more styles of elegant writing, and more designs of beautiful flourishing and ornamental work, than you can find in any other collection in the world.

The Self-Instructor is complete in everything in the form of penmanship.

But the great secret why it is so easy to learn to write from the Self-Instructor, is because everything in the whole book is so thoroughly explained that you cannot help understanding all about it. Every letter, every copy and every ornamental design, is explained by itself in such a plain and simple way that everybody who can read cannot help seeing just how to do it himself. For example, if you want to make any kind of a flourished bird, the Self-Instructor shows you just how to do it. It shows you just how to begin, how to proceed, and how to finish the bird. And so it is with all the plain and ornamental writing. Every copy is thoroughly explained. Nothing has been neglected. Everything that you can find in the Real Pen-Work Self-Instructor is thoroughly explained, and made so plain, simple and easy, that you cannot possibly fail to understand it all, and you cannot fail to learn to write an elegant hand in a very short time, if you will try.

No matter how difficult writing may naturally be to you, you can learn from the Self-Instructor, in only a few weeks, to write and draw just as well as any of the specimens contained in this book, that have been inserted to show the improvement that others have made. There is no more doubt about it than there is that the sun rises and sets.

KNOWLES & MAXIM, General Book Publishers,

Publishers of the Real Pen-Work Self-Instructor in Penmanship,

PITTSFIELD, MASS.

This is a specimen of my writing and the above is a specimen of my flourishing and pen drawing, after five weeks practice from the Real Pen-Work Self-Instructor in Penmanship.

Dave T. Morgan.

WONDERFUL IMPROVEMENT.

The work on this page shows what Mr. Morgan learned to do after only five weeks' practice from the Real Pen-Work Self-Instructor in Penmanship.

It must seem wonderful to a person who never saw the Self-Instructor, that any one could learn to write so well, and do such nice work in so short a time. A short time ago Mr. Morgan was only an ordinary writer. Now, after only a few weeks' practice from the Real Pen-Work Self-Instructor, he has learned to be, as the above work shows, one of the most elegant writers and finest ornamental penmen in the whole world! Such Wonderful Improvement must seem more like a fairy dream than a reality to any one who never saw this Self-Instructor. But the fact is, it is easy enough to learn to write well when you have the proper instruction. A person needs to be shown how. The Self-Instructor tells you all about it. It is the greatest means ever known for learning to write an elegant hand.

HOW TO SIT AT THE DESK

—AND—

HOW TO HOLD YOUR PEN.

A correct position at the desk, and also for holding the pen, are indispensable to good penmanship. The following directions and instructions should be carefully heeded. As the first act of a person in preparing to write is to take a position at the desk, this demands our first attention. It is a noticeable fact that in all occupations there is some one position of the body better adapted than any other to each particular kind of work; and this is particularly true in regard to penmanship. As all written forms correspond to the movements that produce them, beautiful and symmetrical letters can be formed only by free and regular movements; and such movements depend upon those of the muscles of the arm, hand and fingers, which are chiefly connected in the production of written forms. That position which gives the muscles a free and easy action is best suited to the purpose. It is impossible to assume a free and easy position while using a desk or table that is not of the proper height. The height of table or desk is best, at which a person, when sitting in an erect position, with the feet placed firmly upon the floor, and the elbow on the desk, finds that his shoulder is neither elevated nor depressed. After thus preparing yourself, the next thing that requires the attention is the manner of holding the pen; there is no point in penmanship demanding closer attention than this. The demand arises from the fact that beginners almost invariably hold the pen improperly, and that it is one of the most difficult things to learn; yet care and patience will soon bring about the desired result, and when the correct position is once thoroughly fixed there is no danger of losing it. We present the following method for holding the pen, which our experience in teaching has given us ample reason to believe to be the most practicable: Take the pen in the hand between the thumb and the first and second fingers, in such a manner that the holder shall cross the first finger just above the knuckle joint. Let the second finger drop below the first so that the holder shall cross it at the root of the nail. The third and fourth fingers should curve beneath the hand and rest upon the nails. This is the most natural method for holding the pen, for when at rest the hand invariably assumes this position. With these directions and the help of the accompanying cuts, the student cannot fail to acquire a correct position as readily as with the assistance of an experienced teacher.

There are four principal movements used in writing. The *finger*, the *slide*, the *muscular* and the *whole-arm* movements.

The following exercises are arranged according to a new method, and it requires but very little practice with the help of the instructions given under each exercise to get perfect control of all the movements.

By a little practice on these exercises, it is a very easy matter to learn to write.

It is easy enough to learn to write an elegant hand if you have the proper instruction ; these exercises and the following analysis of all the letters tell you all about it.

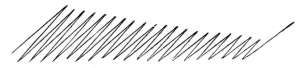

Exercise for Practice on the Finger Movement.

This movement is made by the fingers alone. It is so natural to make letters with the fingers that this movement requires but little attention.

Exercises for Practice on the Slide Movement.

This movement is a motion of the arm from the elbow without moving the joints of either the fingers or wrist. Rest the arm on the muscle near the elbow and the hand on the ends of the last two fingers.

Exercises for Practice on the Finger and Slide Movements Combined.

These are illustrations of the way in which all the short letters should be practiced. Use the slide movement as much as possible while practicing on these exercises, for you are sure to use the fingers enough.

Exercise for Practice on the Muscular Movement.

This movement is produced by rolling the arm on the muscle just below the elbow, without moving the joints of either the fingers or wrist. Move the fingers, hand and arm altogether as one. This movement is always combined with the finger movement, but it is only the muscular movement that requires attention, for the fingers will take care of themselves.

Exercise for Practice on the Finger, Slide and Muscular Movements Combined.

Make the first line with the slide movement, the body of the letter with the finger movement, then finish by throwing a curved line over and around the letter with the muscular movement.

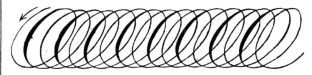

Exercises for Practice on the Finger, Slide and Muscular Movements, also Shading Exercises.

Exercises for Practice on the Finger, Slide and Whole-Arm Movements.

This is one of the very best exercises. A very little practice on this exercise will produce wonders. A person will sometimes get control of all the movements in this exercise by practicing five minutes.

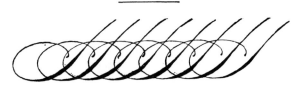

Exercise for Practice on the Whole-Arm Movement.

This movement is produced by moving the whole arm from the shoulder, resting only the hand on the ends of the last two fingers. In making large flourished capitals and doing all kinds of off-hand work, this movement is the best.

Exercise for Practice on the Capital Stem.

The capital stem is the most important principle used in making capital letters, and it is one of the very best exercises for practicing on the whole-arm movement.

Exercise for Practice on Direct and Indirect Oval, also Shading Exercise.

This exercise is adapted for practice on either the muscular or whole-arm movement.

ANALYSIS.

We give on this and the following six pages a complete analysis of all the letters. Every letter of the whole alphabet is taken all to pieces, one at a time, and thoroughly analyzed and explained by itself, in such a plain and simple way, that you cannot help seeing and understanding all about it. You can see at once just how each letter is made. No one ever fails who tries to learn to write from this method. All succeed far beyond their expectations. Even the dullest scholar can learn to write well from this method in a very short time. Do not fail to study carefully the instructions given on this and the following six pages. You will be surprised that you can learn to write an elegant hand so rapidly and easily.

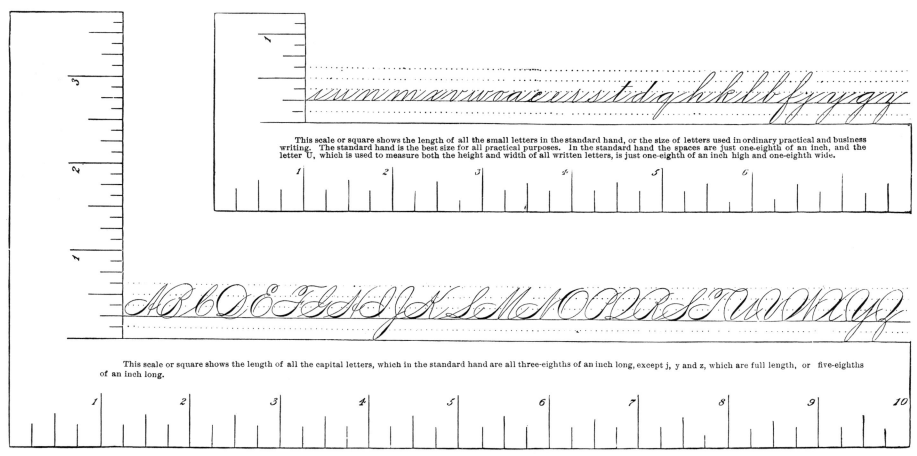

This scale or square shows the length of all the small letters in the standard hand, or the size of letters used in ordinary practical and business writing. The standard hand is the best size for all practical purposes. In the standard hand the spaces are just one-eighth of an inch, and the letter U, which is used to measure both the height and width of all written letters, is just one-eighth of an inch high and one-eighth wide.

This scale or square shows the length of all the capital letters, which in the standard hand are all three-eighths of an inch long, except j, y and z, which are full length, or five-eighths of an inch long.

Copyrighted 1882, by the Publishers, KNOWLES & MAXIM, Pittsfield, Mass.

Scale Showing How Much to Slant Letters.

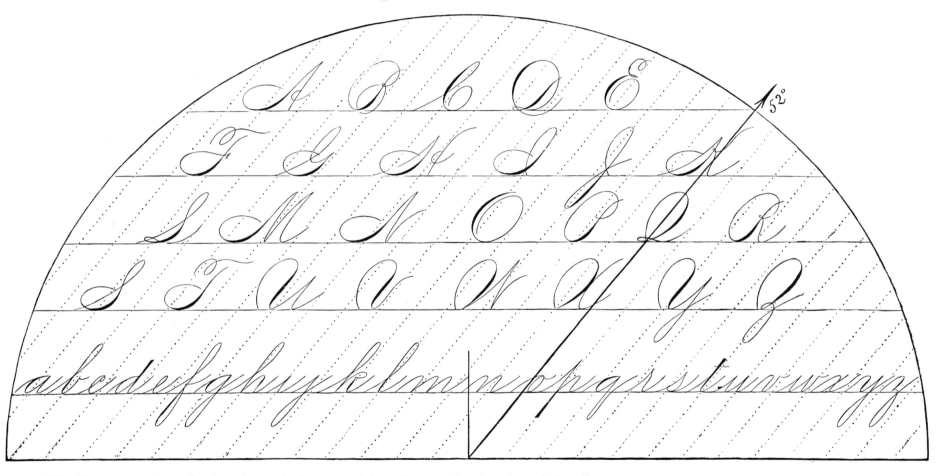

When letters are put together to make words they must all have the same slant in order to look well.

All good penmen agree that letters look the best when slanted about 52° (fifty-two degrees) from the horizontal, the same as you see them in the above cut.

By comparing the letters with the scale of slant, the same as you see in the above cut, you will see at once just how much to slant all the letters.

How much to slant letters is one of the first and most important things to learn. By the use of the above cut and these instructions, it is also one of the easiest things to learn, for you can see at once, without any trouble at all, just how much to slant letters.

Copyrighted 1882, by KNOWLES & MAXIM, Publishers, Pittsfield, Mass.

Principles and the Capitals A, N, M, T, F and K Thoroughly Analyzed and Explained.

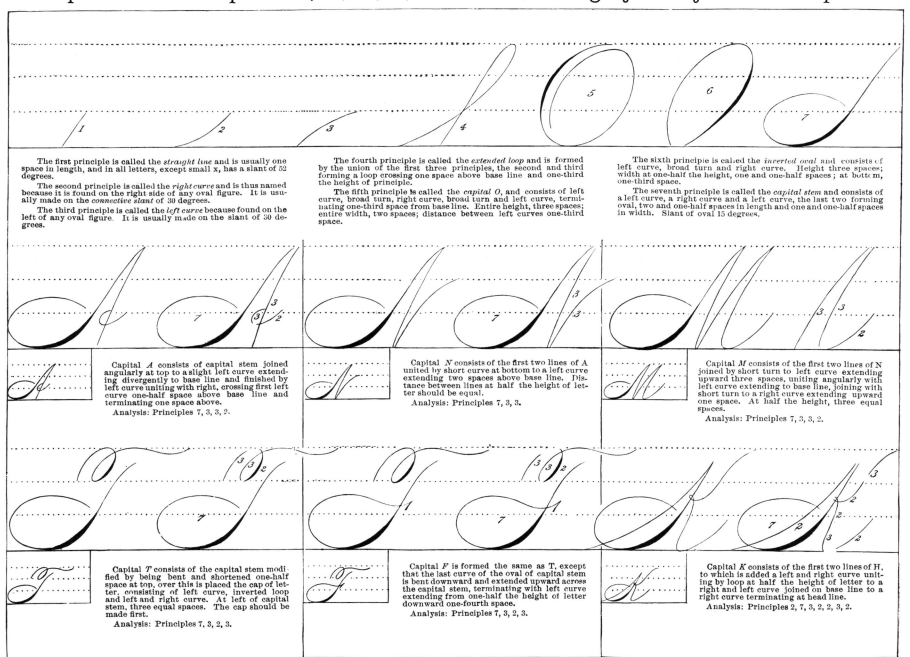

The first principle is called the *straight line* and is usually one space in length, and in all letters, except small x, has a slant of 52 degrees.

The second principle is called the *right curve* and is thus named because it is found on the right side of any oval figure. It is usually made on the *connective slant* of 30 degrees.

The third principle is called the *left curve* because found on the left of any oval figure. It is usually made on the slant of 30 degrees.

The fourth principle is called the *extended loop* and is formed by the union of the first three principles, the second and third forming a loop crossing one space above base line and one-third the height of principle.

The fifth principle is called the *capital O*, and consists of left curve, broad turn, right curve, broad turn and left curve, terminating one-third space from base line. Entire height, three spaces; entire width, two spaces; distance between left curves one-third space.

The sixth principle is called the *inverted oval* and consists of left curve, broad turn and right curve. Height three spaces; width at one-half the height, one and one-half spaces; at bottom, one-third space.

The seventh principle is called the *capital stem* and consists of a left curve, a right curve and a left curve, the last two forming oval, two and one-half spaces in length and one and one-half spaces in width. Slant of oval 15 degrees.

Capital *A* consists of capital stem joined angularly at top to a slight left curve extending divergently to base line and finished by left curve uniting with right, crossing first left curve one-half space above base line and terminating one space above.

Analysis: Principles 7, 3, 3, 2.

Capital *N* consists of the first two lines of A united by short curve at bottom to a left curve extending two spaces above base line. Distance between lines at half the height of letter should be equal.

Analysis: Principles 7, 3, 3.

Capital *M* consists of the first two lines of N joined by short turn to left curve extending upward three spaces, uniting angularly with left curve extending to base line, joining with short turn to a right curve extending upward one space. At half the height, three equal spaces.

Analysis: Principles 7, 3, 3, 2.

Capital *T* consists of the capital stem modified by being bent and shortened one-half space at top, over this is placed the cap of letter, consisting of left curve, inverted loop and left and right curve. At left of capital stem, three equal spaces. The cap should be made first.

Analysis: Principles 7, 3, 2, 3.

Capital *F* is formed the same as T, except that the last curve of the oval of capital stem is bent downward and extended upward across the capital stem, terminating with left curve extending from one-half the height of letter downward one-fourth space.

Analysis: Principles 7, 3, 2, 3.

Capital *K* consists of the first two lines of H, to which is added a left and right curve uniting by loop at half the height of letter to a right and left curve joined on base line to a right curve terminating at head line.

Analysis: Principles 2, 7, 3, 2, 2, 3, 2.

Copyrighted 1882, by the Publishers, Knowles & Maxim, Pittsfield, Mass.

The Capitals H, P, B, R, G and S Thoroughly Analyzed and Explained.

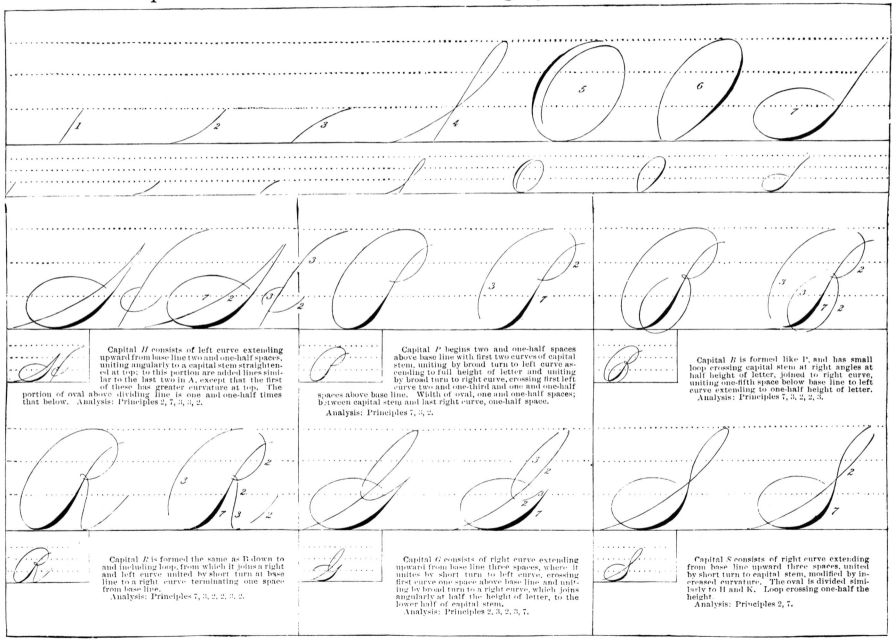

Capital *H* consists of left curve extending upward from base line two and one-half spaces, uniting angularly to a capital stem straightened at top; to this portion are added lines similar to the last two in A, except that the first of these has greater curvature at top. The portion of oval above dividing line is one and one-half times that below. Analysis: Principles 2, 7, 3, 3, 2.

Capital *P* begins two and one-half spaces above base line with first two curves of capital stem, uniting by broad turn to left curve ascending to full height of letter and uniting by broad turn to right curve, crossing first left curve two and one-third and one and one-half spaces above base line. Width of oval, one and one-half spaces; between capital stem and last right curve, one-half space.
Analysis: Principles 7, 3, 2.

Capital *B* is formed like P, and has small loop crossing capital stem at right angles at half height of letter, joined to right curve, uniting one-fifth space below base line to left curve extending to one-half height of letter.
Analysis: Principles 7, 3, 2, 2, 3.

Capital *R* is formed the same as B down to and including loop, from which it joins a right and left curve united by short turn at base line to a right curve terminating one space from base line.
Analysis: Principles 7, 3, 2, 2, 3, 2.

Capital *G* consists of right curve extending upward from base line three spaces, where it unites by short turn to left curve, crossing first curve one space above base line and uniting by broad turn to a right curve, which joins angularly at half the height of letter, to the lower half of capital stem.
Analysis: Principles 2, 3, 2, 3, 7.

Capital *S* consists of right curve extending from base line upward three spaces, united by short turn to capital stem, modified by increased curvature. The oval is divided similarly to H and K. Loop crossing one-half the height.
Analysis: Principles 2, 7.

Copyrighted 1882, by the Publishers, KNOWLES & MAXIM, Pittsfield, Mass.

The Capitals L, I, J, O, E and D Thoroughly Analyzed and Explained.

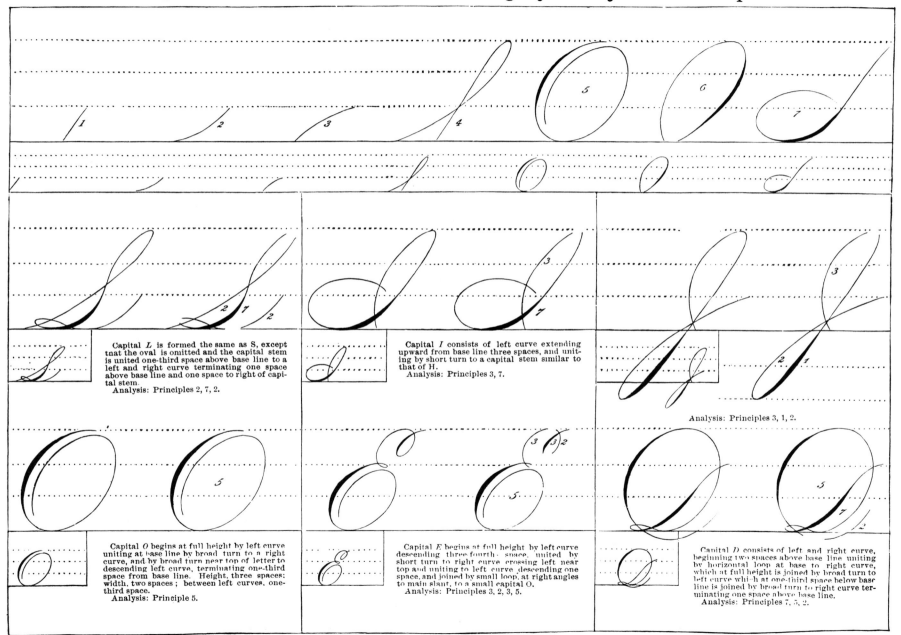

Capital L is formed the same as S, except that the oval is omitted and the capital stem is united one-third space above base line to a left and right curve terminating one space above base line and one space to right of capital stem.
Analysis: Principles 2, 7, 2.

Capital I consists of left curve extending upward from base line three spaces, and uniting by short turn to a capital stem similar to that of H.
Analysis: Principles 3, 7.

Analysis: Principles 3, 1, 2.

Capital O begins at full height by left curve uniting at base line by broad turn to a right curve, and by broad turn near top of letter to descending left curve, terminating one-third space from base line. Height, three spaces; width, two spaces; between left curves, one-third space.
Analysis: Principle 5.

Capital E begins at full height by left curve descending three-fourth space, united by short turn to right curve crossing left near top and uniting to left curve descending one space, and joined by small loop, at right angles to main slant, to a small capital O.
Analysis: Principles 3, 2, 3, 5.

Capital D consists of left and right curve, beginning two spaces above base line uniting by horizontal loop at base to right curve, which at full height is joined by broad turn to left curve which at one-third space below base line is joined by broad turn to right curve terminating one space above base line.
Analysis: Principles 7, 5, 2.

Copyrighted 1882, by the Publishers, KNOWLES & MAXIM, Pittsfield, Mass.

The Capitals C, X, W, Q, Z, V, U, Y, and the Character & Thoroughly Analyzed and Explained.

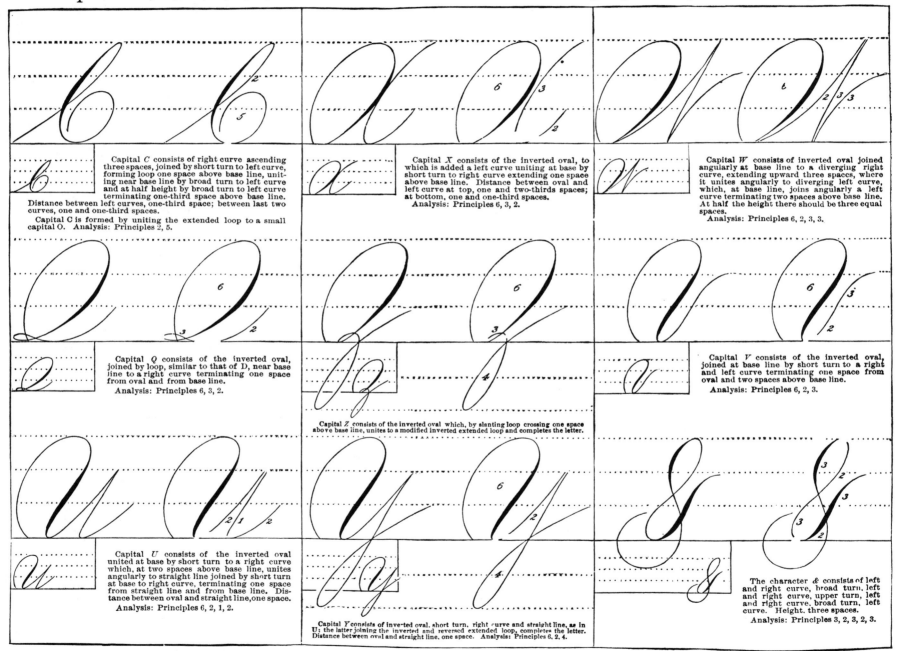

Capital C consists of right curve ascending three spaces, joined by short turn to left curve, forming loop one space above base line, uniting near base line by broad turn to left curve and at half height by broad turn to left curve terminating one-third space above base line. Distance between left curves, one-third space; between last two curves, one and one-third spaces.

Capital C is formed by uniting the extended loop to a small capital O. Analysis: Principles 2, 5.

Capital X consists of the inverted oval, to which is added a left curve uniting at base by short turn to right curve extending one space above base line. Distance between oval and left curve at top, one and two-thirds spaces; at bottom, one and one-third spaces. Analysis: Principles 6, 3, 2.

Capital W consists of inverted oval joined angularly at base line to a diverging right curve, extending upward three spaces, where it unites angularly to diverging left curve, which, at base line, joins angularly a left curve terminating two spaces above base line. At half the height there should be three equal spaces. Analysis: Principles 6, 2, 3, 3.

Capital Q consists of the inverted oval, joined by loop, similar to that of D, near base line to a right curve terminating one space from oval and from base line. Analysis: Principles 6, 3, 2.

Capital Z consists of the inverted oval which, by slanting loop crossing one space above base line, unites to a modified inverted extended loop and completes the letter.

Capital V consists of the inverted oval, joined at base line by short turn to a right and left curve terminating one space from oval and two spaces above base line. Analysis: Principles 6, 2, 3.

Capital U consists of the inverted oval united at base by short turn to a right curve which, at two spaces above base line, unites angularly to straight line joined by short turn at base to right curve, terminating one space from straight line and from base line. Distance between oval and straight line, one space. Analysis: Principles 6, 2, 1, 2.

Capital Y consists of inverted oval, short turn, right curve and straight line, as in U; the latter joining the inverted and reversed extended loop, completes the letter. Distance between oval and straight line, one space. Analysis: Principles 6, 2, 4.

The character & consists of left and right curve, broad turn, left and right curve, upper turn, left and right curve, broad turn, left curve. Height, three spaces. Analysis: Principles 3, 2, 3, 2, 3.

Copyrighted 1882, by the Publishers, Knowles & Maxim, Pittsfield, Mass.

All the Small Letters Thoroughly Analyzed and Explained.

The first principle is the straight line.

The second principle is the right curve.

The third principle is the left curve.

The fourth principle is the extended loop, it is formed of the first two principles, as follows: Upward right curve three spaces, turn, and downward straight line crossing right curve one space from base line. This principle is one-half space wide and three spaces high.

The letter I consists of upward right curve one space high, downward straight line to ruled line, upward right curve, dot one space above letter.
Analysis: Principles 2, 1, 2.

The letter U consists of the three lines of I with a repetition of the last two lines. It is one space high and one space wide and is used for measuring both the height and width of all written letters.
Analysis: Principles 2, 1, 2, 1, 2.

The letter W consists of the letter U changed by making the third right curve one-half space nearer the straight line, and finish with a horizontal right curve.
Analysis: Principles 2, 1, 2, 1, 2, 2.

The letter E consists of upward right curve, downward left curve, crossing right curve one-third space from base line, turn, upward right curve.
Analysis: Principles 2, 3, 2.

The letter C consists of upward right curve, downward left curve one-sixth curve, downward left curve, upward right curve.
Analysis: Principles 2, 3, 2, 3, 2.

The letter R consists of upward right curve one and one-fourth space, downward left curve, downward straight line, upward right curve.
Analysis: Principles 2, 3, 1, 2.

The letter S consists of upward right curve one and one-fourth space, downward compound curve, upward right curve.
Analysis: Principles 2, 3, 2, 2.

The letter N consists of upward left curve, downward straight line, upward left curve, downward straight line, upward right curve.
Analysis: Principles 3, 1, 3, 1, 2.

The letter M is the same as N with a repetition of the last two lines.
Analysis: Principles 3, 1 3, 1, 3, 1, 2.

The letter V consists of upward left curve, downward straight line, upward right curve, horizontal right curve.
Analysis: Principles 3, 1, 2, 2.

The letter X consists of the last two lines of M with a straight line made upward on a slant of 40 degrees crossing first straight line at half the height.
Analysis: Principles 3, 1, 2, 1.

The letter O consists of upward left curve, downward left curve, upward right curve, horizontal right curve.
Analysis: Principles 3, 2, 2.

The letter A consists of upward left curve, downward left curve, upward right curve, downward straight line, upward right curve.
Analysis: Principles 3, 3, 2, 1, 2.

The letter T consists of upward left curve, downward straight line, upward right curve, horizontal straight line, one and a half spaces from base line.
Analysis: Principles 2, 1, 2.

The letter D consists of upward left curve, downward left curve, upward right curve, downward straight line, upward right curve.
Analysis Principles 3, 3, 2, 1, 2.

The letter Q consists of the first three lines of A combined with downward straight line, upward compound curve. Analysis: Prin. 3, 3, 2, 1, 2, 3.

The letter P consists of upward right curve, downward straight line, upward left curve, downward straight line, upward right curve.
Analysis: Principles 2, 1, 3, 1, 2.

The letter L consists of upward right curve, turn, downward straight line, upward right curve.
Analysis: Principles 4, 2.

The letter B consists of upward right curve, turn, downward right curve, horizontal right curve.
Analysis: Principles 4, 2, 2.

The letter H consists of upward right curve, turn, downward straight line, upward left curve, downward straight line, upward left curve.
Analysis: Principles 4, 3, 1, 3.

The letter K consists of upward right curve, turn, downward straight line, upward left curve, downward compound curve, upward right curve.
Analysis: Principles 4, 3, 3, 2, 2.

The letter J consists of upward right curve, downward straight line, turn, upward left curve.
Analysis: Principles 2, 4

The letter G consists of upward left curve, downward left curve, upward right curve, downward straight line, turn and upward left curve.—Prin. 3, 3, 2, 4.

The letter Y consists of upward left curve, downward straight line, upward right curve, downward right curve, upward left curve.—Prin. 3, 1, 2, 4.

The letter Z consists of upward left curve, downward right curve, downward right curve, upward left curve.
Analysis. Principles 3, 2, 4.

The letter F consists of upward right curve, turn, downward straight line, turn, upward right curve, upward left curve.
Analysis: Principles 4, 4, 2.

Copyrighted 1882, by the Publishers, Knowles & Maxim, Pittsfield, Mass.

A B C D E F G H

J K L M N O P Q R

S T U V W X Y Z

a b c d e f g h i j k l m n o p

q r s t u v w x y z & 1234567890

SPENCERIAN SCRIPT.

A Atlanta B Bangor C Cutlers

D Detroit E Esquire F Fulton

G Grafton H Huxley I Ironton

J Johnson K Kentucky L London

M Motley N Natchez O Orths

Copyrighted 1880, by Ivison, Blakeman, Taylor & Co , New York.

P Pindar   Q Quarts   R Richard

S Sundry   T Trenton   U United

V Virgils   W Weights   X Xingu

Y Yazoo   Z Zachary   & Company

Albany. N.Y.   Boston. Mass.   Canton. O.

REMARKS.—This page and the preceding page are specimens of *real written* copies, by Spencerian Authors, who are known the world over as the best **writers that** ever lived. These very pages are the best written pages in the world. They are the best specimens of elegant writing ever done with a pen. These two **pages are taken** by permission from the New Spencerian Compendium of Penmanship, published in five parts, by Ivison, Blakeman, Taylor & Co., New York. The New Spencerian Compendium illustrates to perfection the great skill of the Spencers, and the immense value of their system. Copyrighted 1880, by Ivison, Blakeman, Taylor & Co.

PROMISSORY NOTES.

$4298

New York Nov. 15. 1866.

At Sight, pay to James H. Campbell, or order, Forty two Hundred and Ninety eight Dollars, value received.

Williams & Packard.

C. T. Bainbridge & Co.

445 Broadway New York.

$1700

New York Oct. 3. 1866.

Six months from date I promise to pay Wm. M. King Jr. or order Seventeen Hundred Dollars value received

Thomas Hunter.

A LETTER OF FRIENDSHIP.

Boston, Mass, May 10, 1882.

My Dear Mother,

I wish I could be at home to night. Tell little Nellie I am going to bring her a nice doll.

You spoke Mother, about my improvement in writing They have introduced the Real Pen Work Self Instructor in this school, and this is a fair specimen of my improvement after only four weeks practice.

We expect a vacation in two weeks so I can be at home. Isn't it nice Mother?

The bell is ringing so good bye

From your obedient and loving son,

Frank Spencer.

A BUSINESS LETTER.

Chicago Ill, June 20, 1882.

Messrs Knowles & Maxim
Dear Sirs:— Enclosed find bank draft for three hundred and twenty five dollars, for which send me Real Pen Work Self Instructors in Penmanship

I never expected to find anything that would sell like this book Everybody buys it I would not exchange my agency for the best farm in the state. When I first began to canvass for the Self Instructor I was sick with the dyspepsia, had no money, and could scarcely write so it could be read

Now after canvassing for this book, working in the open air for only three months, I have got entirely well, have made more money than I ever expected to make in so short a time, and this letter is a specimen of my writing after a little practice from the Self Instructor.

Gentlemen please accept my hearty thanks for furnishing me such a pleasant, healthy, and profitable business.

Very respectfully, Your Agent,
Chas. R. Howard.

Go forth, thou little volume,
I leave thee to thy fate ;
To love and friendship truly
Thy leaves I dedicate.

Go forth, thou little volume,
I leave thee to thy fate;
To love and friendship truly
Thy leaves I dedicate.

The purest treasure
Mortal times afford,
Is spotless reputation.

The purest treasure
Mortal times afford,
Is spotless reputation.

On the broad highway of action
Friends of worth are far and few,
But when one has proved her friendship,
Cling to her who clings to you.

On the broad highway of action
Friends of worth are far and few
But when one has proved her friendship,
Cling to her who clings to you.

What's the use of always fretting
At the trials we shall find
Ever strewn along our pathway—
Travel on, and never mind.

What's the use of always fretting
At the trials we shall find
Ever strewn along our pathway—
Travel on and never mind.

On this leaf, in memory prest,
May my name forever rest.

On this leaf, in memory prest,
May my name forever rest.

If you wish to laugh
Glance at my autograph.

If you wish to laugh
Glance at my autograph.

As sure as comes your wedding **day,**
A broom to you I'll send ;
In *sunshine*, use the brushy **part,**
In *storm*, the other end.

As sure as comes your wedding day:
A broom to you I'll send:
In sunshine use the brushy part.
In storms the other end.

Man's love is like Scotch **snuff—**
You take a pinch and that's enough.
Profit by this sage advice,
When you fall in love, think twice.

Man's love is like Scotch snuff
You take a pinch and that's enough
Profit by this sage advice
When you fall in love, think twice

Fee simple and simple fee,
And all the fees in tail
Are nothing when compared to **thee—**
Thou best of fees—fe-**male.**

Fee simple and simple fee
And all the fees in tail
Are nothing when compared to thee
Thou best of fees—fe-male.

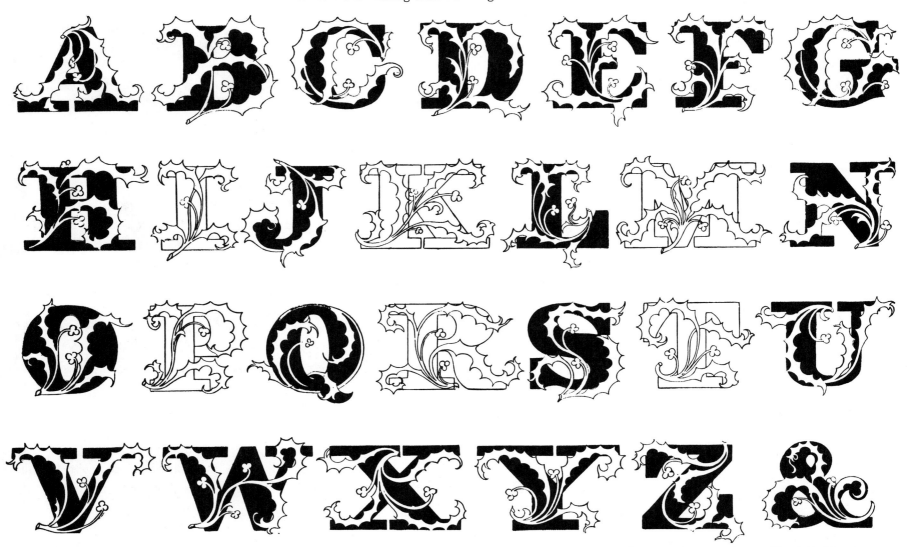

Full instructions for making these Letters given in the Transfer Process.   Copyrighted 1882, by the Publishers, KNOWLES & MAXIM, Pittsfield, Mass.

The Transfer Process.

INSTRUCTIONS

—IN—

THE TRANSFER PROCESS.

The Transfer Process has for a long time been known to leading penmen and pen artists. It has always been kept a sort of secret. It is the quickest and best way in the world to make an exact copy of any kind of ornamental pen-work.

The Transfer Process is so simple, plain and easy, that a child can make an exact copy of any kind of ornamental pen-work, and do it to wonderful perfection.

The Self-Instructor is the only work ever published, which teaches this immensely valuable and important Process, in connection with penmanship.

DO NOT FAIL!

Be sure to read these instructions over very carefully, then you will know all about this Process, and will see and understand for yourself, how it is that you, or anybody, can do such nice pen-work without any trouble at all, and right from the very start. Take a slip or sheet of transparent transfer paper, and place it on the picture to be copied; then with a good lead pencil trace all the outlines and shadings of the entire picture, until you have taken a complete and perfect outline of the original drawing on your transfer paper.

After you have done this, turn your transfer paper over and black the whole other side of it with your pencil. Then place your transfer paper, blacked side down, on your drawing paper, or where you wish to make your drawing, and take a hard fine-pointed lead pencil and trace over all the outlines and shadings of the entire picture. Thus you print in pencilings a perfect

copy of the entire picture on your drawing paper. After you have done this, it is a very easy matter to finish the picture with pen and ink, by putting ink on in place of the pencilings, and shading according to the shading of the original, erasing the pencil marks with a rubber after the ink is put on.

Now this is all there is to it. This is all you have to do to work by the Transfer Process, which you see is very easy.

If you have read these few instructions carefully, you can now sit right down and make an exact copy of any of the drawings in the Self-Instructor, and do it so nicely and perfectly that you will astonish yourself, and astonish everybody else who does not know about the Transfer Process.

You see that all the art or skill that is required to draw anything, is to get the construction lines, or the outlines and shade lines that make up the picture. By the Transfer Process all you have to do is to transfer the lines that make any picture on your transfer paper, with a pencil, and then transfer the pencil picture to your drawing paper. The designs on this page, are perfect Photo-Electrographs, from real pen and ink drawings, made by the Transfer Process, from designs in the Self-Instructor.

The Transfer Process is certainly the greatest means ever invented, or heard of, for making an exact copy of pen-work.

TRANSFER PAPER.

As it is sometimes difficult to get a good article of Transfer Paper, we have decided for the convenience of those who use the Self-Instructor, to furnish the very best quality of Transfer Paper for just what it costs us, which is six sheets for 25 cents. We send six full sheets for 25 cents post paid. Send postage stamps in payment.

KNOWLES & MAXIM, Publishers,
PITTSFIELD, MASS.

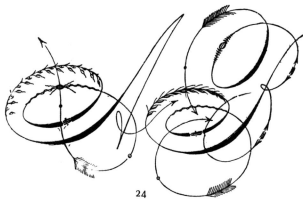

INSTRUCTIONS AND REMARKS.

The above is a picture of the eminent D. T. Ames, the great penman, Editor of the Penman's Art Journal, 205 Broadway, N. Y., sitting at his desk flourishing. He is one of the greatest and most eminent penmen in the whole world. He executed all the work on this page. He flourished it all right off, in a few minutes. This portrait was taken while he was doing the work, and you can see how he sits and how he holds his pen, just the same as you could if you were in his office looking at him.

It is easy enough to do all this work if you sit and hold your pen in the right position. The above picture of Prof. Ames shows how he sits and holds his pen, when actually at work. You can learn to sit and hold your pen in the same position by looking at his picture, just as well as you could if you had Prof. Ames himself right with you to show you how.

After you once get the correct position, it requires but very little practice to be able to do all this kind of work.

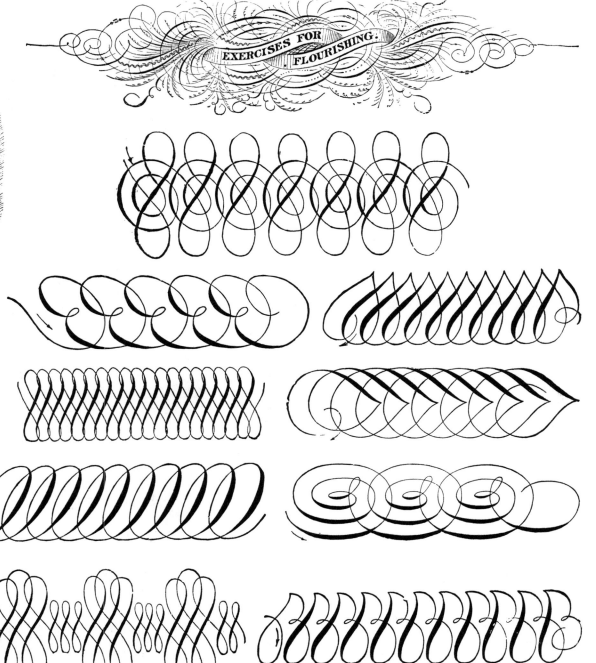

GENERAL INSTRUCTIONS IN FLOURISHING.

In flourishing reverse your pen and hold it with the point toward you, and strike the lines with the whole-arm movement, resting only on the finger nails, turning your paper to correspond with each stroke. Above we give a pattern bird and its analysis; all birds are usually made on the same general plan.

In flourishing a bird, strike the parts in the order in which they are given above.

The point of beginning and direction of the movement is indicated by the arrow. The line forming the tail must be continued so as to form the body, breast and underbill of the bird at a continuous sweep, without a change in the position of the pen or hand. The remainder of the bill and the top line of the head are best made by changing the pen to the direct position, the same as when writing.

Where the leg joins the body, a slight erasure may be made in the body stroke, but if the outline of the body remains unbroken it is not especially objectionable. In striking the tail and surrounding flourishes, reverse the sheet so as to have the bottom from you, holding the pen in a reversed position.

The above cuts are a perfect photo-electrograph from the real pen work. They were designed and flourished to show the quickest and easiest way to learn to make an elegant flourished bird. Any one can see that it must be a very easy matter to learn to make the different parts of the above bird, and anybody can also see that it is easy to combine the different parts and so make the bird; therefore it is very easy to make the bird. Anybody, even the dullest scholar, can make an elegant flourished bird by a little practice from the above copy. All that is necessary is to sit down and try. You will be astonished to see how easy it is.

INSTRUCTIONS.

This page shows you just how to make different kinds of birds. It shows how to begin, how to proceed, and how to finish a bird. This page was designed and executed by John D. Williams, and is the greatest means ever known for learning to make all kinds of flourished birds. Taken by permission from Williams & Packard's Gems of Penmanship. Copyrighted 1866, by Williams & Packard.

These copies need no explanations, as they explain themselves. Everything is made so plain and simple, and easy to understand, that you can't help seeing just what to do, and how to make different kinds of birds without any trouble at all.

After 3 months practice.

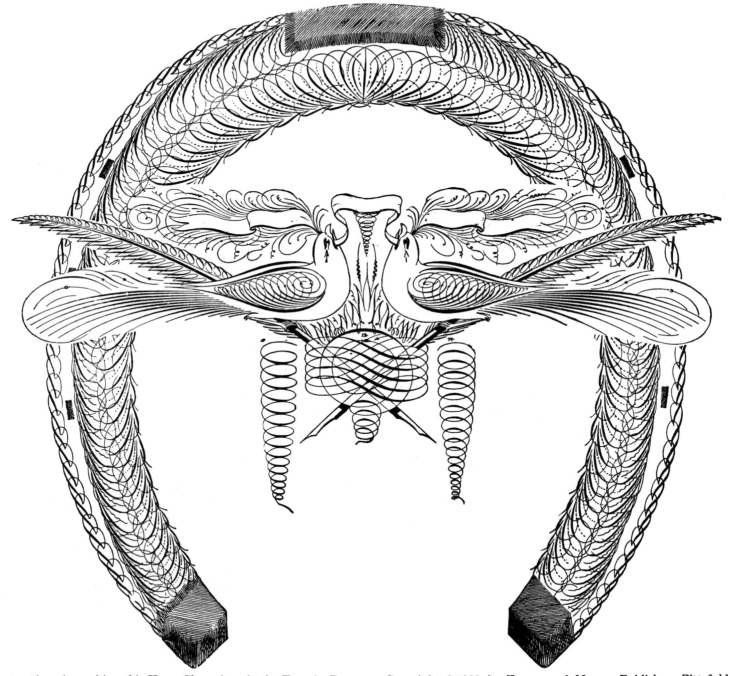

Full instructions for making this Horse Shoe given in the Transfer Process.   Copyrighted 1882, by KNOWLES & MAXIM, Publishers, Pittsfield, Mass.

Photo-Electrographed from Real Pen-Work, by the eminent John D. Williams.   Taken by permission from Williams & Packard's Gems.
Copyrighted 1866, by Williams & Packard.

Full instructions for making this Eagle and Snake given in the Transfer Process.

REAL PEN-WORK LION.

Full instructions for making this Lion given in the Transfer Process. Copyrighted 1882, by KNOWLES & MAXIM, Publishers, Pittsfield, Mass.

REAL PEN-WORK DEER.

Full instructions for making this Deer given in the Transfer Process.   Copyrighted 1882, by KNOWLES & MAXIM, Publishers, Pittsfield, Mass.

REAL PEN-WORK HORSE.

Full instructions for making this Horse given in the Transfer Process.   Copyrighted 1882, by Knowles & Maxim, Publishers, Pittsfield, Mass.

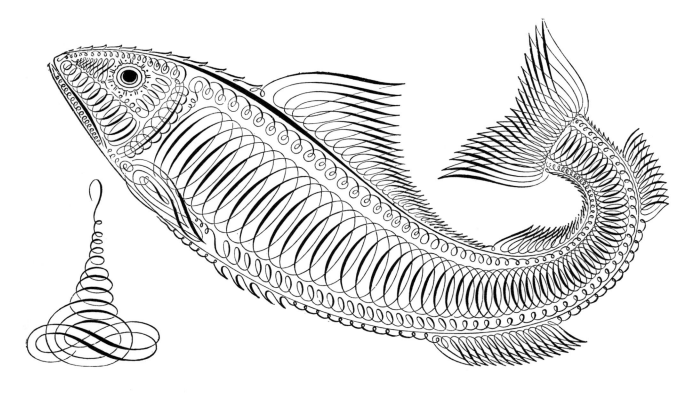

Full instructions for making this Fish given in the Transfer Process.

Full instructions for making these Heads given in the Transfer Process.

RUSTIC ALPHABET

BY D. T. AMES.

Full instructions for making this Design given in the Transfer Process.

Marking Alphabet.

ABCDEFGHIJKLMN
OPQRSTUVWXYZ&
abcdefghijklmnopqrst
uvwxyz.

From Ames' Lessons in Box Marking, Penman's Art Journal.

ATKINSON SIGN PAINTING UP TO NOW

A complete manual of the Art of Sign Painting—Contains Ninty Six Designs or Layouts and accompanying color notes—Seventy Five Alphabets embracing all standard styles, their modifications and alternates—Comprehensive text covering all practical phases of the art—for every day reference in the shop—

By FRANK H. ATKINSON

PUBLISHERS

FREDERICK J. DRAKE & COMPANY

CHICAGO   U. S. A

PREFACE

Atkinson presents his book without apology and wishes to state that the "work" was not inspired by any latent egotism nor a desire on his part to pose as an author. The intent has been to present his experience of twenty years in as short and concise a manner as possible, omitting nothing that will aid the energetic and determined student to acquire greater knowledge and ability.

There are no "experiments" in the book, the practical and technical matter reflects the methods in vogue with the foremost "talent" of the present day. Nor does he wish to supplant other previous and meritorious works upon the same subject. His advice is, *"Get them all."*

The book as you find it is an every day record of experience and association with foremost contemporary talent. Aside from the designs and alphabets in the book there is no credit due him.

With these few remarks he respectfully dedicates the book to the Craft in general.

He has purposely compiled the text in a rather disconnected way —making it necessary to consult the index at all times. He also repeats some phases under different headings, which he thinks an advantage.

The Reviews and Test Questions in back of the book are for the beginner's guidance and help, if he desires to study closely and systematically. Atkinson feels that the book will be gladly welcomed by the Craft in general. No book extant contains as much text or as many Alphabets.

"HIMSELF."

NO. 2. SWELL DESIGN FOR YOUR CARD.

BY FRED WATRIN, NOTED SIGN PAINTER, OF PORTLAND, ORE.

Copy on 22x28 Bristol Board, using Waterproof India Ink. With
a blue pencil, mark size you wish drawing reduced.

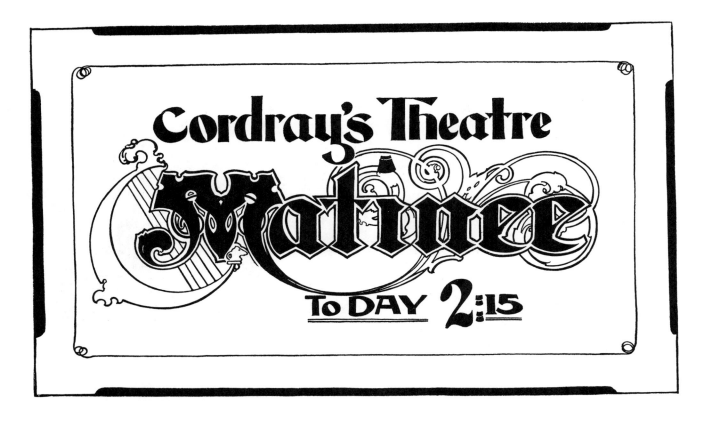

NO. 3.   MATINEE DESIGN

can be used large or small on Oil Cloth, Muslin or Board.   For board use a background of pale lemon yellow—for the harp and scroll use rich old gold color—not too strong, just enough to show distinctly.   "Cordray's Theatre" gets gold with a black outline. "Matinee" do in gold with double outline of black and vermilion (black next to letter) for "today 2:15" use gold with tuscan red outline, for matt line and bevel use gold.

CHAS. ARNOLD,
Sign Painter

No. 4. SUGGESTION FOR BUSINESS CARD.

Copy on 22x28 Bristol and have Zinc Etching made the size you desire.

No. 5. STATIONERY IN ART NOUVEAU STYLE.

Original by Chas. J. Strong, head of Detroit School of Lettering
and a recognized leader in the art of lettering and design. Slightly
varied in minor detail to suit general use. Copy 22x28 Bristol Board.

No. 6. DESIGN FOR DEPARTMENT STORE.

(INTERIOR DISPLAY.)

Make Board in "tablet" style with an extremely wide bevel, at least 6 inches—with rounded corners, prepare in the usual manner and gild entire surface solid gold or bronze, including the bevel —produce design in one color of dark purple flock.

No. 8. A TEMPORARY DISPLAY IN BOARD, MUSLIN, OR OIL CLOTH PANEL.

For entire scroll use Gold Bronze, "break on" the word "Holiday," in very pale bluish green and "cut in" with dark bottle green. On the word "Sign" do the outline and broken shade in black, fill center of letters with Lt. Eng. Vermilion, leaving white show as it appears in the design. Fill balance of design in pale greenish yellow—use same color deepened a little with Chr. green and umber (enough to render it distinct on the yellow), for the irregular Vertical Bars. Get these Bars all parallel with irregular distances between, also make Bars in different widths, to give design a "snappy" look.

48

No. 11. MUSLIN OR OIL CLOTH.

ATKINSON.

Do "Cigars" in rather deep old gold with wide outline of Tuscan. On circle use pale, rich blue strong enough to show well, leaving white show as in design, giving poster effect. Center of Circle *very* pale grey. Little panel at top in pale sienna, deepen a trifle for outline and matt on same; letter it straight burnt sienna; streamer at bottom, same. Balance of lettering, deep purple.

No. 12. HOLIDAY MUSLIN OR OIL CLOTH.

ATKINSON.

"Headquarters for"—dark olive. Shield Panel very pale olive green with dark olive outline and matt line. Letter "for Xmas" dark blue. Initial Panel in medium pink, leaving "T" white with vermilion outline. Nouveau Scroll at top, deeper pink. For matt inside of scroll and panel use pale emerald green; same on Laurel Sprig; deepen for outline on Sprig. Balance of "Toys" light vermilion. Imported Novelties in dark olive.

No. 14. MUSLIN OR OIL CLOTH.
ATKINSON.

"Break on" The Curio Shop, in pale chr. green, extra light in tone. "Cut in" rather dark warm olive green. "Returns" on panel in pale lemon. "Poster Floral" in vermilion; detailed in light pink. On small lettering do all caps in vermilion; rest of lettering dark bottle green.

No. 15. OIL CLOTH OR MUSLIN.

ATKINSON.

Little Panel at top in pale and deep Brewster green. The Sprig in bright emerald green, rather pale; detail same in darker tone of same color. "Teco" use medium dull purple (tuscan red and ultramarine), and for outline, deepen same color; outside outline in pale greenish yellow. Wreath Panel pale greenish yellow with dark olive ground. Streamer two shades of pink. Art Pottery light and deep vermilion, using the deep for high light.

No. 16. MUSLIN OR OIL CLOTH.

ATKINSON.

Do "B" and scroll surrounding in extremely pale old gold. A broken shade of tuscan on "B." Balance of "Books" in deep vermilion with black high light. Ribbon panel, pale warm grey. Detail in medium purple grey; letter, deep olive green. Long panel at top gets pale bluish green border and scroll. White letter "cut in" deep bluish green.

No. 17.   DESIGN FOR "CUT OUT" SWING, LARGE OR SMALL.

ORIGINAL BY FRED WATRIN, NOTED SIGN PAINTER, PORTLAND, ORE.

Make pattern and "black in" layout (will save bother in execution). Perforate for pounce—will also answer for the carpenter. In cutting, follow extreme outside outline for shape of swing; leave the rest solid and work up design per following.

Do all lettering white with gold outline. Ground of sign, dark old gold. Scrolls pale old gold, outlined in pale med. chr. yellow. Black "wave" scroll do in tuscan red. Border on oval in gold "white inset."

No. 18. DESIGN FOR BOARD ARM SIGN—SCROLL SAWED.

ORIGINAL BY J. P. ZIRNGIEBEL OF PORTLAND.

Do scrolls and "circle" panel at top in solid silver. Background rich deep chocolate; border pale chocolate; lettering silver; pale sienna high light; tuscan red slant shade. Firm name letter in reds.

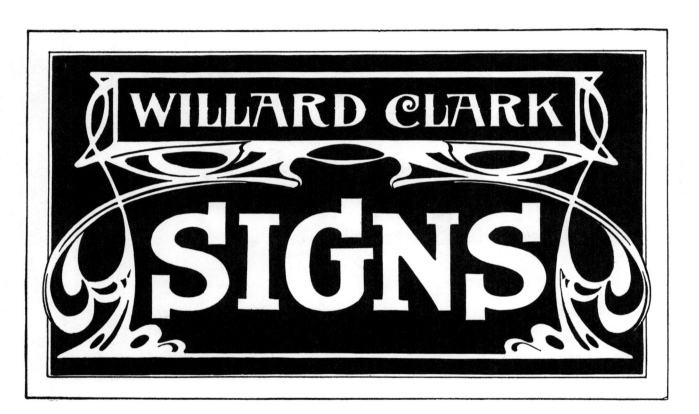

No. 19. COLOR BULLETIN.

AFTER ORIGINAL IDEA BY JESSE WADDEL, PORTLAND, ORE.

Do the "nouveau" design in medium old gold, with a heavy "poster" outline of darker old gold. Ground outside of design in deep chocolate. Ground of name panel medium bluish green, white letter. Ground signs panel deep orange, toned strong with burnt sienna; white letter wide poster outline, of tuscan. Red border, white inset.

NO. 20. DESIGN FOR LARGE OR SMALL PANEL.

ATKINSON.

Panels on end solid gold; lettering on same in black. "Signs" panel, very deep rich vermillion ground. Word "signs" in gold, heavy black outline. Border on "signs" panel, light vermillion. Fine line on border in black. Main border on design in medium old gold. Outside fine line medium yellow. Wide line and two fine lines "split" on main border in tuscan red. Main ground, deep chocolate color; letter in gold.

No. 21. DESIGN FOR DRUM SIGN.

AFTER W. H. ABBOTT, NOTED "MODERN" OF NEW YORK CITY.

Do the background in deep burnt umber. Matt or border in medium rich old gold. Matt line, medium rich blue inclined to paleness. "Signs" panel, tuscan red ground, gold border. The word "Signs" XX gold, outline of pale vermillion. Firm name panel, pale gold. Firm name, rich old gold; white outline. Scroll, pale gold. Small lettering on main ground, deep gold. Number at top, white, gold outline; ground, deep vermilion. Narrow panel behind scroll and firm name panel in black.

No. 22.   DESIGN FOR PANEL BETWEEN WINDOWS.

ATKINSON.

Do the background in deep warm drab, and do side border and back panel (running full length) in still deeper drab. Do "leaves" in rather medium dull grass green; detail in very bright pale tint of emerald green. Do "poster" blooms in pale purple; deeper purple for detail—panel at top; pale medium yellow border; deep "tan" ground, white letter; tuscan outline. Panel at bottom same as top panel. "Oval" deep vermilion ground, white letter, pale English vermilion border.

No. 23. DESIGN FOR BOARD PANEL.

AFTER JESSE WADDELL, PORTLAND, ORE.

Background pale terra cotta; borders in deeper shades of same color. Small letter panels top and bottom of design in deep warm gray, letter white, black outline. "Signs" panel in deep rich blue; pale blue scroll with medium blue outline. "Signs" white letter, black outline; inside fine line medium gray.

C.S.FORINGTON CO.

COMMERCIAL

SIGN PAINTERS

BANK AND OFFICE LETTERING.

No. 24. DESIGN FOR WINDOW.

ATKINSON.

Do all detail in panel in burnish gold, deep XX, stipple remainder of panel and gild, deep gold XX. Burnish gold outline all lettering and stipple centers; gild in deep gold. "Sign painters" gets blend shade of reds; split carmine. Do "stops" black and deep chocolate; blend "Vandyke" brown to medium Harrison's 1793 vermilion. Center or background of panel do in transparent "putty pounce," balance of lettering rather wide outline of black.

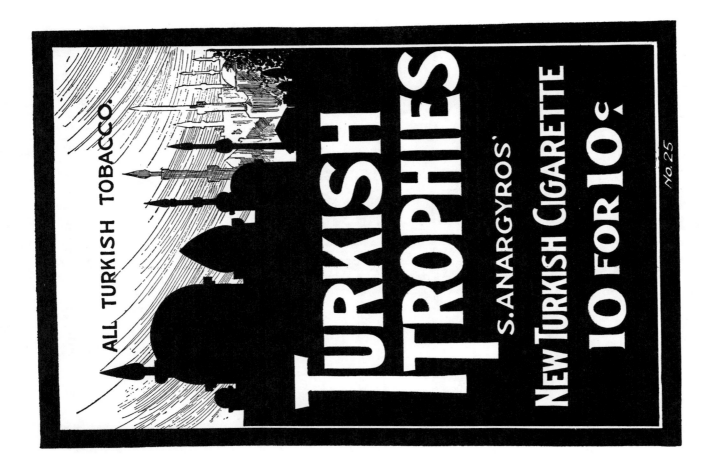

NO. 25. DESIGN FOR WALL OR BULLETIN.

AFTER E. W. DAVIS, OF GUNNING SYSTEM, CHICAGO.

Use blend of medium and orange yellow in the sky; carry same color around for inset. Form silhouette and background in deep rich purple, leaving white letter "middle distance" pale purple; "far distance" in *very* pale purple. Border on sign light vermilion.

No. 26. DESIGN FOR BULLETIN.

AFTER LAWRENCE MAZZANOVICH, FAMOUS CHICAGO SIGN PAINTER

Make from heavy poster board and mount face with muslin or blank white paper. Ovals and Scrolls do as shown in gold bronze; outline them in pale buff; letter in dark bottle green. Panel in center, deep vermilion ground, white letter; pale vermilion outline.

No. 27. SPECIAL BULLETIN.

FROM DIRECT PHOTO, BY JOHN' COLENUTT, FAMOUS THROUGHOUT THE U. S.

Background dark olive green. "Manhattan Theatre" is white letter with red outline. On panel do borders and ground in pale bluish greens. Letter the panel in straight Prussian Blue. Wreath goes two tones of rather pale buff. Ground of wreath dark vermilion with white letter. Do the inset and vertical bars in pale lemon. Do scroll in medium old gold, cut in roughly, leaving white relief line as shown. Border on sign bright red.

No. 28. DESIGN FOR BULLETIN OR STORE SPACE.

AFTER A. R. HUSSEY, CHICAGO SIGN PAINTER.

Rococo panel gets red ground, white letter, black outline. Rococo scroll in pale bluish green. "Corsets" in very deep bottle green, black inset. Border medium olive green, white inset.

No. 30. BULLETIN.

BY JACK COLENUTT.

Drawing made from photo of same.

Main ground very pale olive green. Small lettering upper right hand corner in dark bottle green. Firm name in white, heavy black outline. Start scroll on circle lower left hand in deep olive "break blend" to real light in the ending. Ground of circle deep old gold blended to medium buff, white letter black heavy outline. Panel in medium dull purple, white letter, red outline, hang with pink ribbon. Address in black. Border in medium olive with white inset.

No. 29. BULLETIN OR STORE SPACE.

AFTER LARRY MAZZANOVICH, FAMOUS CHICAGO SIGN PAINTER AND LITHO DESIGNER.

Do background in pale emerald green. Do both panels deep olive green ground, white letter, red outline, black shade. Borders on panels deepen emerald color a trifle, and for "trim" and scroll in borders make it still deeper. Wreath in medium grass green, darken for detail, and use the deepened color to "cut in" word "The." Do the "Torch" in medium old gold, model in dark old gold and a little umber and chromo green, and high light in medium yellow. Do vapor from torch in deepened background color. Ribbons in tuscan pink.

No. 31. BULLETIN OR STORE SPACE.

AFTER J. P. ZIRNGIEBEL, PORTLAND, ORE.

Main ground light buff to right of scroll division; same color for panel on left end. Ground back of left end panel in tuscan red. Letter left end panel in red with black outline. "Hop Gold Lager Beer" in medium strong bright yellow. "Cut it in" (form panel also) in tuscan red. Scroll and "matt line" medium old gold. Red border and white inset. For ribbon, deepen the background and detail in red. Letter it black.

NO. 32. BULLETIN OR WALL.

AFTER E. W. DAVIS, WITH GUNNING SYSTEM, CHICAGO.

Bright strong yellow ground. Panel deep rich vermilion, white letter, black outline. Hand and watch natural color. Small lettering in black. Border on sign warm old gold.

NO. 33. BULLETIN.

AFTER VAL COSTELLO, NOTED CHICAGO AND WESTERN SIGN PAINTER, LOS ANGELES.

Do matt in rather pale emerald green; do all the cut stuff on design same color. Panel top and bottom pale bluish green letter, medium olive green ground. Main ground in deep olive green. Script in white with black outline, red shade. Border in deep vermilion.

No. 34. BULLETIN.

AFTER FRANK NICHOLSON, NOTED EXPOSITION SIGN PAINTER.

Ground outside of panel very pale olive green; ground inside of floral border deepen same color a trifle. Floral border in two tones of dull purple (pale and medium). Panel is white letter, black outline, deep vermilion ground. Balance of lettering inside of floral border in deep purple. Small lettering in corners of design in black. Border in strong orange yellow.

No. 35.   SPECIAL NEW YORK BULLETIN.

BY JOHN COLENUTT.

(Drawing made from photo.)

Medium pale buff outside border, inset fine lines lemon yellow, main ground deep rich chocolate, *wide matt* in medium old gold, and ground inside of matt almost straight burnt umber, with little poster floral in tuscan, with tuscan purple rough outline.   Semicircles at top in pale orange, lettered black.   Panel at left, blend of pale old gold to pink and letter black; circle panel pale vermilion band, white letter, deep vermilion ground.   All scrolls in rich pale old gold with medium old gold outline.

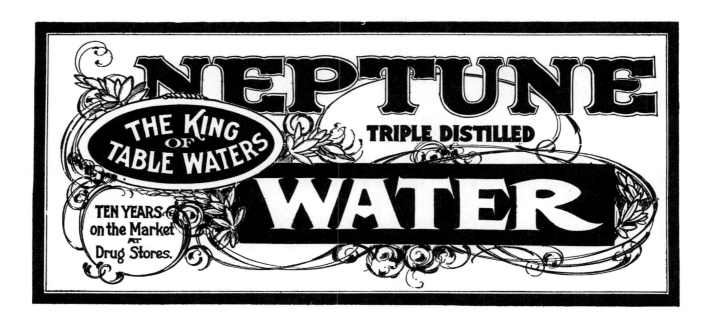

No. 36. BULLETIN.

AFTER HARRY HOAG, FORT WORTH, TEXAS.

Pale, warm green ground. Oval in pale blue letter, deep blue ground, pale blue border. "Neptune" dark bottle green, double outline in same color made lighter in two tones. "Water panel" in red ground, white letter, black outline; small lettering in black. Deepen ground color for "leaves" and do scrolls in greenish gray strong enough to "show." Red border on sign and red, fine line for inset.

NO. 37. BULLETIN.

AFTER G. W. PATE, NOTED SIGN PAINTER OF KANSAS CITY.

Extremely pale burnt umber background. Panel at end gets rich pale bluish green letter "cut in" with deep dull blue. Border on same in rather pale old gold. Cut or outlined trifle deeper old gold. "Zepto" deep vermilion, outline black and inset tuscan red. "Tooth cleaning pencil" deep warm drab, inset black, "cut in" with bright saffron yellow, leaving wide outline of white. "Antiseptic panel" same as end panel. Border in red, white inset.

No. 38. SPECIAL NEW YORK BULLETIN.

BY JOHN COLENUTT.

(Drawing made from photo.)

Background in deep, dull blue. Medium old gold border, and pale old gold inset. Panels in pale saffron with borders in orange, toned rich with burnt sienna. Display lettering in chocolate with tuscan outline; scrolls in pale, bluish green or strong pink. Do the "back" panels in lighter shade of background color. Small lettering in red and black.

NO. 39. BULLETIN.

AFTER WILLARD CLARK, 244 E. MADISON ST., CHICAGO.

Pearl gray matt with borders in vermilion. Panel is black ground, pale, greenish yellow letter with heavy white high light. Scrolls and matt lines in vermilion. Small lettering in black.

No. 40. ROOF BULLETIN.

AFTER A. R. HUSSEY, CHICAGO.

Do background in pale gray, inclined to purple. Do borders and end ornaments light and medium bluish green. Cut in "Automobile" dark bluish green, leaving white letter; give it wide black outline. "Garage" in dark bluish green, medium blue inset, black outline. Balance of lettering deep olive green with black inset. Red borders.

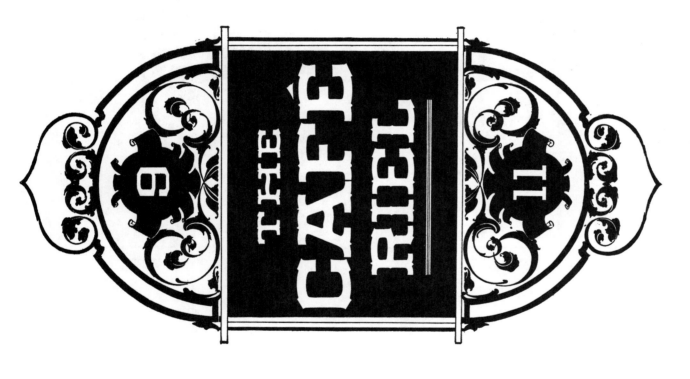

No. 41.   DESIGN FOR DOOR LIGHT (GLASS).

ATKINSON.

Outline entire design and lettering in bright gold. (XX) deep. Stipple scrolls and background and gild in lemon gold. Fill centers of lettering in black. "Open" ground at top and bottom of design do in whiting putty pounce. Wide outline of black around entire outside of design.

CASINO GARDEN

OPENS JUNE 1st

CHANGE of BILL
EACH WEEK

CONCERTS
BY
LEHMANN

Harry B. RICHMON
·SOLOIST·

Marie SUMMERS
·SOPRANO·

No. 42.   FOR OILCLOTH OR MUSLIN.

FRANK S. NICHOLSON.

Do panel old gold ground, pale buff letter. Decorative stuff, pale buff, outlined orange yellow. Casino Garden deep drab, black high light, and pale purple wide "poster outline." Small lettering in black. "Concerts by, etc.," in two bright reds, white or pale gray background.

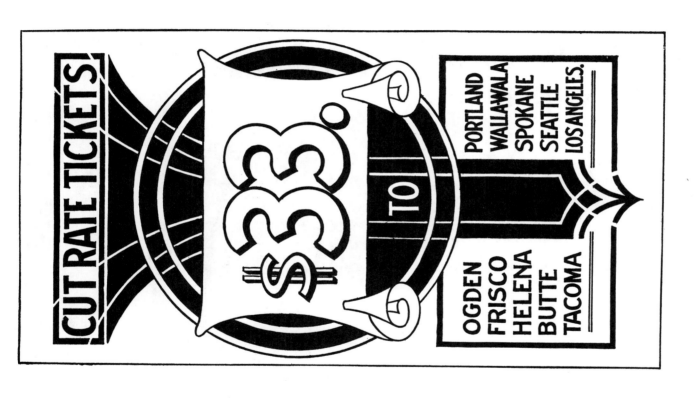

No. 45.   SUGGESTION FOR LARGE SIDEWALK SIGN,
BOARD PANEL OR OILCLOTH

HARRY HOAG.

Do background in rather pale lemon yellow. "Banner" in center, pale orange yellow. Little panel at top in white ground—black lettering. Balance of design rich pale old gold (quite strong), leaving white show on circles and stripes as in design. Panel at bottom, white ground, with red letter. "$33" pale English vermilion, outlined and shaded in deep Harrison's vermilion.

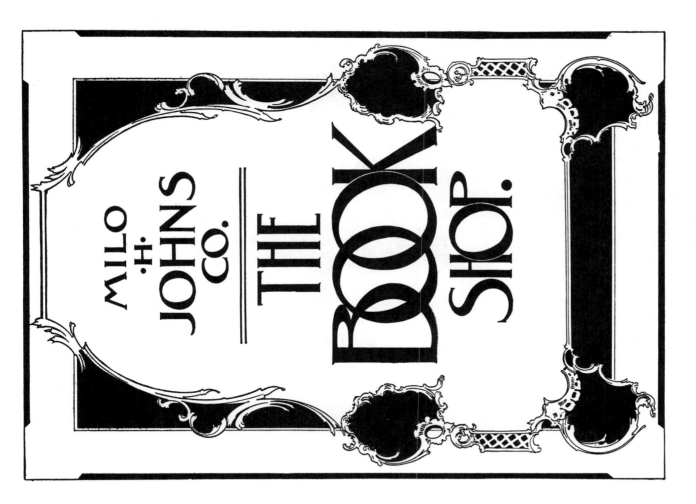

NO. 43.   DRUM, SMALL PANEL OR TABLET.

ATKINSON.

Ground of panel solid gold—letter in black.   Matt medium olive green—matt line in silver.   Ground inside of matt deep olive green.   Rococo scroll in lemon gold outlined in pale buff color. "Centers" of scroll at corners and side, fill in deep oxidized copper.

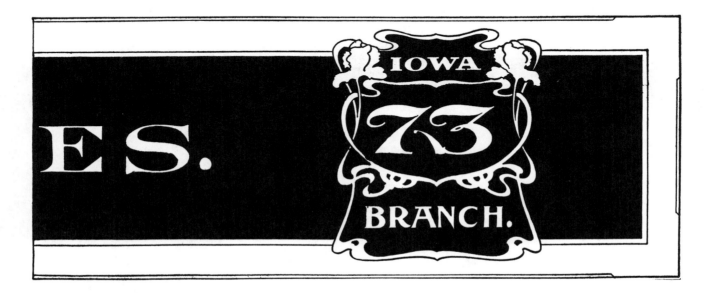

No. 44. ART NOUVEAU "END" FOR FASCIA BOARD.

ATKINSON.

Main board, black smalt ground—surface or raised gold letter. Deep olive green matt—gold matt line, panel in gold, top and bottom "cut in" medium rich chocolate—outline gold letter in black. Center of panel "cut in" deep chocolate, black outline on letter.

No. 47. "END" FOR FASCIA BOARD.

Do panel solid silver. Scrolls in white—outline and detail in pale terra cotta, stripe line in black. Main board, silver letter outline tuscan, background in medium rich chocolate, finish in spar varnish.

No. 48. DESIGN FOR SIGN PAINTERS' STATIONERY.

Can be used for Letter Head, Bill Head and Card.

ATKINSON.

Make drawing four times larger than "cut" desired. Have zinc etching made from same.

THE MILLINERY IMPORTING CO.

No. 49. SWELL DESIGN FOR VERY SPECIAL WINDOW.

AFTER HARRY BRIDWELL, CINCINNATI, OHIO.

Do entire detail of design and outline on lettering in burnish XX deep gold. Heavy stipple on solid parts of design, and gild XX deep gold.

Note.—The solid black on design is clear glass. Fill lettering solid black.

No. 50. DESIGN FOR WINDOW.

AFTER ED. MILLS, PORTLAND, ORE.

Burnish silver outline on lettering and scrolls. Do border in solid silver. Fill lettering in deep rich blue. Shade lettering in neutral tint of ground color. Fill scroll in stipple silver. Rather deep tone of pale rich blue on matt, and do the background in stipple of very pale warm lead color.

No. 51. WINDOW DESIGN.

Outline lettering heavy, in medium rich blue and frost centers in white. Shade with same color, trifle lighter. Do Nouveau border in rich pale blue, and stipple ground in rich pale terra cotta tone.

No. 52. WINDOW DESIGN.

ATKINSON.

Outline entire design in burnish gold XX deep. Fill all small lettering deep old gold color, stippled. Fill "Grant's Printery" stippled lemon gold. Split shade of black and dark warm olive green. Stipple centers of "Printing" pale buff, wide outline of tuscan on same, with slant shade of black. Put in ground of panel in deep warm olive green. Fill border and scrolls stippled lemon gold. Putty stipple space each side of number panel. Outline the number in black and put in ground of deep vermilion.

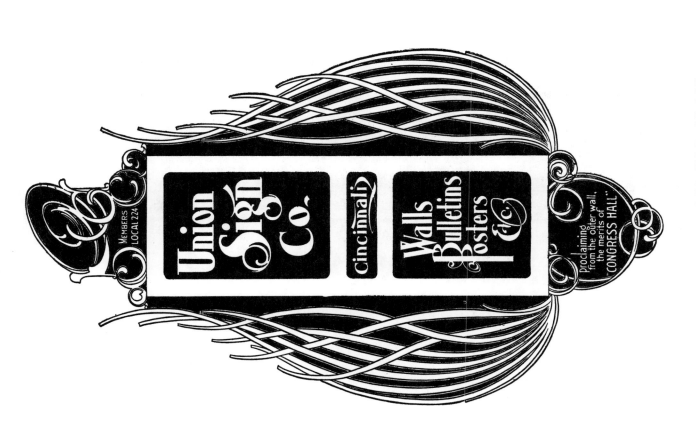

NO. 54. NARROW PANEL FOR GLASS.

AFTER FRANK QUEILE, NOTED SIGN PAINTER OF CINCINNATI, OHIO.

Outline entire design, lettering included in XX deep burnish gold. Stipple lemon gold on border of panel. Fill design outside of panel in nice tone of warm yellowish green, rather pale. Background of panel in deep rich peacock green. Black outline on lettering, and stipple centers in white. Main ground of sign in deep rich purple. For matt line, use medium purple, strong enough to show on ground color. Fill sprigs at side in rich old gold color.

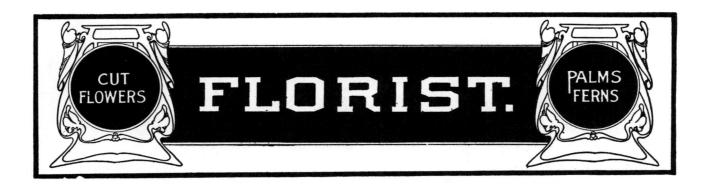

No. 53. GLASS PANEL FOR BOTTOM OF WINDOW—
OXIDIZED COPPER FRAME.

G. W. PATE, K. C.

Outline all detail in panels in burnish gold, stipple and gild in
same gold. Lettering in panels, outline gold XX deep, stipple centers, and gild lemon gold. "Florist," burnish gold outline, stipple
lemon gold centers. Deep chocolate ground.

No. 55. WINDOW.

FRED WATRIN, PORTLAND, ORE.

Burnish outline of gold, wide "varnish line" inside carried close to outline, and do all insetting in varnish. Fill "Balls" different colored bronzes. Black outline, and split shade of black and warm chocolate quite deep in tone.

No. 56. WINDOW DESIGN.

AFTER FRANK S. NICHOLSON

Line whole design in XX deep gold, and outline all lettering in deep gold. "Sporting Goods," stipple center, and gild lemon gold; double color outline of black and red, black next to letter. Fill space above oval panel in deep vermilion, stippled. Lettering in side panels, fill in black, and outline the letter in black at the same time. Ground of side panels in pale warm buff, stippled. Firm name gets stippled deep gold, with double color outline of black and red. Fill between fine lines in design in rich medium bluish green.

No. 57. SCROLL SUPPORT FOR "BOX" FASCIA.

BY ATKINSON.

Blend flat surface in pale tones of olive green, old gold and pink, also pale rich purple. Do "Returns" in red blend. Scrolls, medium old gold, shade and high light. Letter convexed in black and warm gray, outline in XX deep gold leaf.

No. 58. "CAP."

BY ATKINSON.

Convex in two tones of rich blue. Do scroll in pale terra cotta, edged in lower tone of same color. Pale warm gray ground.

No. 59. "CAP."

BY ATKINSON.

Do the "convex" in light and deep vermilion. The scroll in medium old gold or pale green. Edge in lower tone of either color. White or pale yellow ground.

ESTABLISHED 1870.

ALLAWAY & HANCOX

SIGNS

2540=2542 COTTAGE GROVE AV.

PHONE SO. 1058.

SIGN HANGING.

CHICAGO.

No. 60. FOR BUSINESS CARD OR SIGN.

BY ATKINSON.

For "Window" work up in black and gold, using lemon gold stipple in lettering and scroll centers.

No. 62. "CAP."

BY HI MOTT ALLEN, OF BUFFALO.

Scroll added by Atkinson.

Blend letter from deep red to pale vermilion (starting at bottom).
Outline and shade in black. Scroll in pale greenish yellow, edged in
medium olive green. Ground of panel deep olive. Border of panel
same as scroll. Pale yellowish green ground on sign.

No. 63. PANEL.

BY G. W. PATE, K. C.

Engraved from original drawing.

"Atkinson" white letter, wide light blue outline with deep blue edge. Background in very pale rich, blue. "Panel" in medium rich chocolate with vermilion poster "gags" in it. Small letter in rich blue, white outline "cut in" poster style. Border, rich red with white inset.

—OR THIS—

"Atkinson" pale English vermilion, wide white outline. Ground pale yellowish green. "Panel" modeled in deep green. Small lettering straight tuscan red with white poster outline. Red border, white inset.

No. 64. PANEL.

BY G. W. PATE, K. C.

Engraved from original drawing.

"Signs" deep rich red, wide poster outline in pale English vermilion with broken fine-line in deep red. "Splits" in lettering pale
vermilion. Wreath in light yellowish green. "Cut in" center of
"S" tail dark warm green, outline wreath same color. "The Hello
Kind" in bright green, strong enough to show well on white. Scrolls
in pale old gold or light pink.

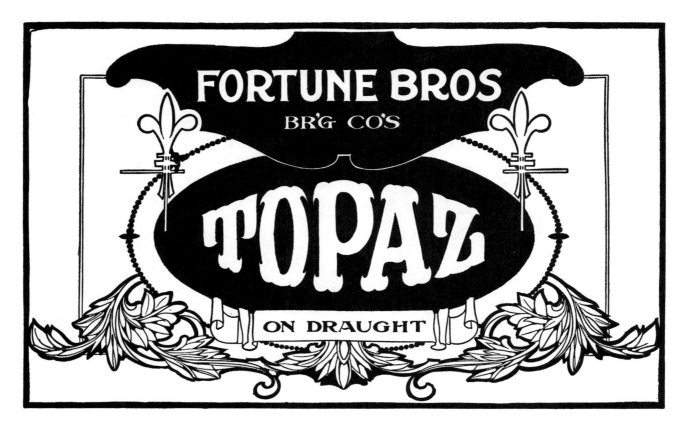

No. 65 PANEL.

M. D. PRICE, CHICAGO.

Top panel tuscan red ground, gold letter, black outline. Oval panel get deep chocolate ground, medium tone of terra cotta for border and gold leaf for beads. "Topaz" wide outline of gold, saffron yellow for center, and a heavy edge of black. Scroll in medium old gold, detailed in deeper tone of same color. Ribbon at bottom, solid gold leaf. Letter in black. Main ground deep olive green. Matt line pale blue. Matt in medium olive green. Silver bevels.

No. 66. BULLETIN LARGE OR SMALL.

M. D. PRICE, CHICAGO.

"Ravinia Park" in dark bottle green, with black inset. Panel gets bright red ground, white letter with black outline. Leaves at sides in bright yellowish green, detail in deeper tone of same color. Panel at bottom in very pale chr. green, letter in black. Ribbons at sides pale lemon yellow, detail in deeper tone of same color. Little panels at bottom in tuscan red. Main ground of sign pale warm grey. Olive green for border.

No. 67. DESIGN FOR SMALL PANEL.

HENRY THIEDE, CHICAGO.

Background and matt in two rich tones of citron yellow. Panels and scrolls in warm deep tones of slate color, detail in black. Lettering in gold leaf outlined in rich vermilion.

No. 69. TABLET FOR INTERIOR DISPLAY.

ATKINSON.

Medium slate color ground. Do poster scape in black, also "brush" at bottom. Letter in gold leaf. Lemon gold leaf bevel or border.

No. 72. POSTER BY VAL COSTELLO.

From original drawing.

Background in pale buff. "Art Students League," red with white inset. Porte crayons in old gold. Tube at top in white. Color from tube very deep purple. Lettering top and bottom in black. Matt and bars in deeper tone of ground color. Border citron yellow.

No. 77. SMALL PANEL.

ATKINSON

Do side scrolls in dark olive, touches of gold high light on them.
Do panel scroll lemon gold leaf, outlined in black. Do the EYE
natural color, lettering deep gold leaf. Black ground varnish.

No. 74. DESIGN FOR CARDS.

HI MOTT ALLEN, OF BUFFALO.

Black and white same as plate.

No. 79. SWING SIGN.

BY F. H. SOWDEN, BURLINGTON, IA.

Black and gold.

No. 80. DISPLAY SHOW CARD.

Gold bronze scroll, panel at bottom in deep vermilion, white letter, black, outline. Main ground of card mottle in pastel crayons, using pale green, pale purple and pale orange. Little panel at top medium bluish green, white letter, black outline. "$15" in black, rest of lettering grass green.

The Royal Dentifrice

That gleam of white behind the lips that gives the smile its chief-est beauty, milady cleans and here's the means that add a pleasure to the duty.

No. 81. SHOW CARD.

Pale gray card, do the scroll in pale blue, letter in very deep blue. Display letter gets outline of pale old gold. Rectangular panel gets ground of pale orange.

No. 82. SHOW CARD

Pale gray card do the "stencil" poster in black. Letter in bright
pink tuscan outline and red inset. Small letter at bottom in red.

No. 85. SHOW CARD.

Use pale gray card, do poster border in black and orange. Letter in pale rich blue. Outline the display line in deep blue.

No. 86. MANOGRAPH DESIGN.

Do ornamental stuff in greenish greys. All lettering in black, with top line outlined in pale emerald. Ellery's Band, outline of red and pale cold grey. Ground of little panel two tones of pale purple. White ground.

MAGDA TOILET CREAM

It's possession lends an air of refinement.

It's use is an indulgence in an ultra-fashion-able luxury.

Drug Dept.

Main Floor

No. 87. SHOW CARD.

Use dark grey card and do all ornamental stuff in pale and deep gold bronze. "Magda Toilet Cream," white with red outline, fill in black roughly on ground inside of gold on upper part of design, do the poster blossoms in red. Two white panels lower left of design in pale olive, letter bright blue. "Drug Dept.," "Main Floor," pale blue, orange border.

No. 88. SHOW CARD.

Use uncoated card and "rub-in" some pale tones of burnt sienna, warm gray and purples, using sofe pastels with cotton pad. Do the stein in warm medium tones of gray and old gold. Panel in pale bluish green, letter in deep olive, border on panel deeper tone of blue green. "Ye Olde Inn Ale" black lower case, Red "Caps."

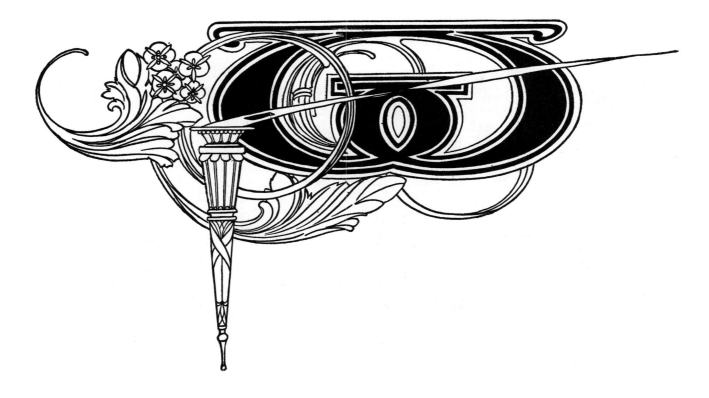

No. 89. INITIAL, GLASS OR BOARD.

GARNER, CHICAGO.

Do the "caps" in double outline of black and gold, fill center in deep vermilion. Do the scroll and torch in bright outline of lemon gold leaf and fill in aluminum bronze.

No. 90. DOOR LIGHT PANEL.

GEO. OLSEN, WITH GUNNING SYSTEM, CHICAGO.

Do the Nouveau border in bright gold outline, stipple center same on lettering—black ground.

No. 92. LETTER HEAD, CARD OR POSTER.

AFTER M. WHELAN, N. Y.

For poster do top line in two tones of old gold, outline and drop shade in tuscan. Do ornamental stuff in pale yellowish grey, and outline it in medium tone of cold old gold. Main panel, blend ground of deep to light vermilion—white letters—black outline. Panel at left of design, pale yellowish green, letters in deep green. Address lettered in black.

No. 93. DESIGN.

BY M. P. KOB, CHICAGO.

Do the ribbon in dull tone of buff, outline and detail same in medium old gold. Lettering in deep vermilion, high light in pale vermilion. Stroke of black on shade side. Do "Figure" in poster style, using abbreviated natural color. White ground.

No. 94. "SWING."

BY M. P. KOB, CHICAGO.

Scroll top in gold color, high lighted and shaded. Blended deep green ground. Main panel, warm, deep orange yellow ground, white letter, with black outline. Rough stroke shade in deep vermilion and carmine. Bevel of panel in pale gray. Small lettering in black.

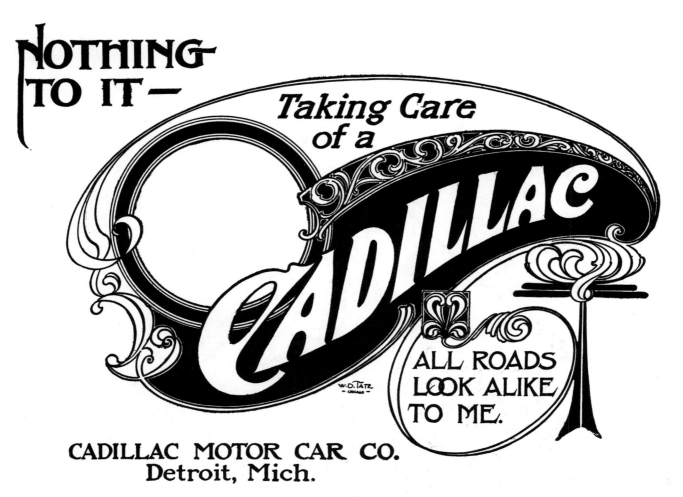

NOTHING
TO IT—

Taking Care
of a

CADILLAC

ALL ROADS
LOOK ALIKE
TO ME.

CADILLAC MOTOR CAR CO.
Detroit, Mich.

No. 96. DESIGN FOR BULLETIN OR WINDOW.

ENGRAVING MADE FROM ORIGINAL DRAWING BY W. D. TATE, NOTED
CHICAGO SIGN PAINTER.

For bulletin do work upon scroll in medium old gold, where detail occurs use deeper tone of same color. Ground inside of scroll at top of design, pale lemon yellow. "Taking Care of" lettered in Tuscan red. Display panel "cut in," using deep rich purple, white letter with wide black outline; also inside wide outline of orange yellow. Lower small panel deep vermilion ground, white letter. Lettering in main ground deep gray with black high light. Main ground in very pale tone of warm gray. Bright vermilion border.